Put God First

Enile Hargett

Put God First - Published in the United States of America by Pastor Enile Hargett ©2021 at Gospel 4 U Publishing

www.gospel4unetwork.com

ISBN: 978-0-692-48686-3

Printed in the United States of America

April 2021

DEDICATION

I would like to thank God for being the head of my life and leading and guiding me through my book. I know this book will help and draw people closer to God. I also would like to thank my children for that extra push that I needed in the process.

ACKNOWLEDGEMENT

I want to thank God who helped lead and guide my hands through this book. I also would like to thank my beautiful children, Gary, Marcus, Brianna, Nyera, Diamond, and Princess Zipporah; they all gave me that extra push I needed to finish my book.

I would like to express my special thanks of gratitude to Apostle Dr. Larry Birchett, Jr., for connecting me with his wife, Pastor Dr. Joanna Birchett, and Gospel 4 U Publishing. Thank you, Gospel 4 U Publishing, for making this dream become a reality. I thank God for showing me in a dream which publishing company He wanted me to use, and that is Gospel 4 U Publishing company. Thank you, Lord!

FOREWORD

My name is Taliah Savage. I've known the author for over 21 years. "Put God First" is written with you in mind. It is a very inspirational book, and I know you will enjoy. This book lets me know that no matter how many times we fall short in life, God will never leave or forsake us.

The character, Matthew, is a good man, but he chose to put money and his job before God and his family. By doing so, he lost everything, his job, his car gets repossessed, and his relationship with his wife and daughter left him, and he became homeless. Even though he losses everything, Jesus sends and places people in his life to help him get back on the right path.

First, He sends the archangel Michael down, which in turn leads him to a church where the angel Gabriel is at. Now since Matthew was homeless, Gabriel lets him stay in a small room that was in the church until he gets back on his feet. He realized who they were when he visited heaven and saw them standing next to God. Finally, on his journey back on the right track, God told Matthew that he was going to use him as His mouthpiece. He is to lead all the lost souls back to Christ. Now once he accepted God back into his life, angel Michael and Gabriel told him their work is done, and they must leave. God also told him, "Don't be afraid. I will always be with you." "Now everything he lost was returned to him, including his family and the love he has for God. Now Matthew and his family preach the gospel on the streets and everywhere they travel. I can relate to this book as well as some of you can also because there are times when we don't always put God first. I can honestly say my life is so much better since I put God first

God Bless

Taliah Savage

CONTENTS

INTRODUCTION

Matthew is a devoted family man who loves the Lord but should've always kept the Lord first in his life.

Matthew's life was going great until he stops putting God first in his life. His life gets turned upside down when he losses everything he owns, including his family. He then eventually meets two friends sent by God, and they help him get back on track but not until Jesus takes him for a visit to heaven and hell.

CHAPTER 1

The love of my life

Matthew loves the Lord, and he is a dedicated church member. He would go to church every Sunday and attend bible study on Wednesdays. Matthew was even the pastor's assistant. They would travel to multiple churches a week to host conference meetings. He even went to Jerusalem to see the tomb where Jesus was laid. Matthew just loves spending time with the Lord. He often fast and prays daily. When church service was over, he would even still be on fire for the Lord and would continue to worship God.

Every morning he would pray, and one of his daily prayers was for God to send him a wife. He wanted a modest wife, not one fancy (worldly woman), and the number one thing he wanted is for her to love God like he does. On September 7, 1986, Matthew was invited to a church revival by his best friend, Jim. The revival was being held at a small church in Atlanta, GA. The church was pretty packed that night. The church had praise dancers and two choirs, and two different pastors speaking that night.

When Matthew was singing and praising the Lord, he noticed a beautiful woman with blonde hair sitting across from him in the pews. She waved at Matthew when she noticed he was looking at her from across the room. When service was over, he decided to boldly go up to her and introduce himself.

"Hello, my name is Matthew, and I couldn't help but notice you across from me," he said. "Hello, my name is Rachael, and it's nice meeting you," she replied, shaking his already extended hand for greeting. Matthew said, "Church service was great tonight." "I agree," said Rachael.

"Do you mind me walking you to your car?" Matthew asked.

Rachael replied with a smile, "Sure, you can." When they were walking, they began to talk about the Lord. Matthew told Rachael he got saved at the tender age of thirteen. Rachael really enjoyed Matthew's company; they decided to take each other's phone number. They couldn't wait to talk to each other so they could be on the phone for hours, and they would even fall asleep talking. On May 5, 1987, Matthew and Rachael exchanged vows and got married.

A year later after they were married, they brought their baby girl, Katie, into the world. Matthew and Rachael were living the perfect and great life together.

Matthew applied for a position as an engineer. Rachael worked as a *secretary* at a law firm. They bought their first home in a very quiet neighborhood downtown Atlanta, Ga. Also, time went on when Matthew began traveling with his boss and co-workers to different states on business trips.

When Matthew would come home from his business trips, he would talk to his wife about his trips. One day when they were eating dinner, Rachael said to Matthew I've been noticing the change in you since you started working at that job. When we first met, you were so dedicated to God, but now you just stopped going to church, attending bible study, and attending the men's fellowship. You just work long hours and constantly go on long business trips.

Matthew raised his voice and said, "I will go to church when I am good and ready. When I make time, I will go." Right now, I am just too busy with work, and besides, we have a big deal closing soon. Racheal, honey, everything is going to go well for us. I am making over $100,000 dollars a year, and we have a nice home that we can call our own. Racheal said, "I don't care about how much money you're making. I just want you the way you used to be when we first met in church. It was once a time when we used to pray together, and we used to have bible study meetings in our home." Matthew said, "There's a time in life when an opportunity comes to you just once, then you have to grab hold of it. This is a once and a lifetime job. I am working at a job I truly finally love; you should be happy and grateful that I have a job. Racheal said, "I want you to get it together, or else I and Katie are leaving and going to stay with my parents." Matthew said, "Just give me a couple of days to think things through." "I will give you just a couple of days, Matthew, but I mean it, and that's it," Racheal replied.

So a couple of days went by, and Matthew was still away on his job's business trip, and Racheal called him to talk about what his plans were concerning them. Matthew said, "Racheal can you give me some more time, please." She immediately said, "No, I gave you plenty of time, Matthew. We are moving out tomorrow, and we will be at my parents' house." Matthew begged Racheal not to leave him, but Racheal had her mind made up, and she was determined that she was leaving Matthew.

The next day she packed her and Katie's belongings and left the house with her car packed. Matthew returned home three days later to find the house empty, and Katie and Racheal's belongings were all gone. Matthew tried calling, but she never answered, and the answering machine kept coming on. After being at her parents' house for a couple of months, Racheal decided to get her and Katie's own apartment that would be closer to her job. Matthew still was going on business trips with his job. His boss even gave him a higher-up position as an executive in his department. Matthew was really happy and enjoying himself until, one day, he came home and was feeling really lonely without his wife and daughter. Matthew had so much pride in his heart. He couldn't even call his wife and Katie and tell them how much he missed them. Matthew just kept on working hard, trying to pretend not to be missing his family.

CHAPTER 2

When Tragedy struck Matthew

On June 2, 1993, tragedy struck Matthew unexpectedly when his boss came into his office. He said, "Matthew, you got a minute. I would like to talk to you about what's been going on here." Matthew said, "Sure, pull up a seat, Richard." Richard said, "I am laying quite a number of people off, and I am sorry I have to lay you off as well. Our company is making cutbacks to save money." So, Richard hands Matthew a pink slip and apologizes to him. We can't afford your salary anymore. I am so sorry we have to go this route. Matthew didn't know what to say at first, but then he said, "I understood. You have to do what you have to do; besides, if I was in your shoes, Richard, I would have done the same thing." "Thanks for understanding me," replied Richard. "No problem, Richard," said Matthew. "You can work here until Friday," Richard turned around and added, "Sorry for any inconvenience this may have caused you."

When Richard left Matthew's office, Matthew couldn't believe what he had just heard. Matthew started thinking about what he was going to tell his wife, and then he started thinking about all the bills he has to pay. *"I have a 1,700 dollar mortgage I have to pay,"* Matthew said to himself. Now, where am I going to find another job? The look on Matthew's face looked like he wanted to crawl under a shell and hide and cry his eyeballs out. Matthew didn't waste any time finding another job. He typed up his resume and searched the internet for another job. He sent out different resumes to quite a few companies. A week went by, and he didn't receive any phone calls or emails. He called one job, and they said, "We will be hiring in about six weeks; check back then." There were other jobs he called, and they said, "Call in a week; we should have something available then." Soon Matthew started feeling depressed because all he was doing was sitting at home doing nothing because he had no job leads. Matthew became so depressed, and he began going back to his old ways of drinking and worrying about what he was going to do financially because it's been four months since he has been without a job. One night he didn't go to bed until 4:00 am because he had been up, crying and thinking about his family. The phone rang that morning, and it was Racheal on the other line. She said, "Hello, Matthew, how have you been?" Matthew said, "Great, and how have you and Katie been doing?" "We were wonderful. I was calling you to see if you have any time today to go with me and Katie to the park." "Well, I will meet you there, and what time did you want to go?" Matthew asked. "We will be there around 3 this afternoon, would that time work for you?" Racheal asked. Matthew replied, "Yes, that sounds great. I can even pack all of us some lunch." "Ok, that sounds great; see you soon." Matthew walked to the park around the corner from his house.

When he arrived, he spotted Katie first and then Rachael's blonde hair. "Daddy!!!" Katie yelled for Matthew and then ran over to him. Matthew picked her up, hugged, and kissed her on the cheek. Then he walked over to Racheal and gave her a hug and a kiss on her cheek. "How have you been holding up, Racheal?" asked Matthew. "I have been doing very well," Racheal said, "you look like you haven't been sleeping at all." "I have, honey; I've just been busy, that's all." Katie Yelled to Matthew to push her on the swing. He was very glad to so that he could avoid any other questions Racheal might want to ask him. Matthew was really enjoying himself so much that he didn't even realize how much he really missed his family. Racheal said, "Come on, Matthew and Katie, come and have a bite to eat. I packed us lunch." Racheal asked Matthew the question that he didn't want to hear, "How's work going for you?" Matthew didn't want to tell Racheal that he lost his job, so he told her, "It's been going great, and I have lots of projects to complete; that's why my face looks this way. I am just tired and need a good night's rest." Racheal told Matthew she received a very good job offer and she was thinking about taking it, and the job was located in Florida. "I would be working in a law office and making double of what I am making here." Matthew said, "How could you accept an offer like that, and what about me. How am I supposed to see Katie? I thought we could drop our differences and get back together." Racheal got really upset with Matthew and said, "I thought you would be happy for me." They both began arguing back and forth with each other, which led Katie to cry seeing her parents arguing. Racheal grabbed Katie and left the park. Matthew Walked away in tears and his heart broken.

When Matthew got home, he got into his car for a quick drive to clear his head. When he was driving, he started thinking about his family and all his bills that he began to receive shut-off notice which he began to avoid. One of the notices he received was a ten-day vacate notice from his mortgage company. It read, "Please vacate within ten days as we gave you sufficient time to vacate the property, if you refuse to vacate the property, the Sheriff will be there to escort you off the property. You will then have ten minutes to gather your belongings and leave the property." Those ten days came very quickly for Matthew.

That next morning the Sheriff arrived at Matthew's door. Matthew opened it up and began begging the officer at the door to give him more time. Matthew told him that he lost his job, and soon as he gets another job, he will catch up on everything. The officer didn't want to hear anything Matthew was saying. Then Matthew heard a truck pull up in his driveway. Matthew looked out of the door, and it was a tow truck backing up in his driveway. He ran to ask what was going on. The man was the repo man coming to get his car for non-payment. Matthew couldn't believe all that was going on. The officer was still waiting at the door, and he gave Matthew time to grab his duffle bags and stuff them with his clothes. After that, Matthew went outside his house while the Sheriff padlocked the door. Matthew called his friend, Jim, and explained to him what was going on. Jim rushed over to Matthew's house to pick him up.

Matthew asked Jim if he could crash at his house until he could find a job and get on his feet. Jim said, "I am sorry, man, but my wife is not having that. She wouldn't even let her baby brother come live with us when he was homeless. What I could do for you is to take you to the shelter downtown. I can help you look for work before I take you to the shelter downtown." Jim took Matthew to a lot of companies to see who was hiring. Everywhere they went, people kept saying they weren't hiring right now. Matthew asked Jim to take him past his old job. They pulled up in the parking lot and got out of the car, and proceeded to go inside the building. Looking from the front door entrance there was not a single car out there besides Jim's. So Jim and *Matthew* decided to look inside the tinted windows.

They saw the building completely empty. Matthew couldn't believe what he was seeing. They got back into the car, and Matthew got his phone and called his old boss to find out what was going on with his old job, but, instead, he just got a recording saying the phone number you have dialed was disconnected. He even dialed some of his other co-workers phones, and their phones said the same message. Matthew started thinking about what was going on. He remembered a while back that one of his co-workers mentioned that the job was going to be in another state soon. Matthew never really paid any attention because he always played and joked around, and nobody took him seriously. "They moved and never let me know. I believe they planned this and just got rid of me. I wonder," Matthew said in a sad voice like he wanted to cry. Jim and Matthew arrived at the shelter in downtown Atlanta. Jim said, "Call me, man." Matthew said, "I will," with his head dipped into his chest and a very sad look on his face. Matthew went into the shelter's lobby doors, and the lady at the desk said "Hello, how may I help you, sir?" Matthew said, "Ma'am, I need a place to stay." She said, "I am sorry, sir, but we are booked up for the night. You can try back tomorrow if you like. You have to come early, around 7 pm sharp, that's the time everyone starts lining up. We have people here every day come and go." Matthew said, "Ma'am, I have nowhere to go. What am I supposed to do?" The lady said, "Sir, I am sorry, but you can try other local shelters." Matthew said, "I don't have a car or a ride." Matthew was so angry he just stared out of the building's window.

Matthew said thank you to the lady and left the building, and started walking down the street, worrying about where he was going to sleep. So as Matthew began to walk down the street, he saw this man with whitish hair. The man approached Matthew with some pamphlets that talked about the return of Jesus, and the other pamphlets talked about Jesus loves you. Matthew took both of the pamphlets and read the front of them, and said to the man, "If Jesus loves me, why am I going through so many hardships, and why am I homeless?" The man said, "My name is Micheal, and your name is?" "Well, my name is Matthew, sir." Matthew was still upset; you can hear in his voice as he spoke. "Do you know Jesus?" Michael asked. Matthew replied, "Yes, I do." Micheal said, "Jesus is the only one that can get you out of your situation. Our father knows everything about us." Matthew said, "Sir, it's been nice chatting with you, but, you see, sir, I am trying to find somewhere to lay my head before the storm comes. Besides, I am not trying to get wet." So Matthew walked away from Micheal. The clouds moved in, and the sky was darkened. It began to rain. Matthew ran under this vacant bakery that has been closed down for years. There was a hole over the storefront, and he became soaking wet. Matthew laid down with his jacket covering his shoulders up, and as he sat down, he began to cry out to the Lord, "God, I am so sorry for whatever I did to You and my family. God, I know I was angry towards You, and didn't do what I was supposed to do. Lord, I am begging You to fix my life back like it was. Fix it, Lord, Please!!! I won't leave You again, Lord. This doesn't feel good, Lord. I feel so alone out here with nobody on my side to help me out. I left You, Lord, and I know You would never leave me. Matthew soon fell off to sleep.

CHAPTER 3

My walk with Jesus

In Matthew's dream, he saw Jesus and Micheal walking together coming towards him. The only thing Micheal had that was different to him was wings that stood out, and they had such a glow to them. They were so bright that they looked just like the sun and were pretty white. Jesus said to Matthew, "I heard you called upon my name." Matthew answered Jesus and said, "Yes, I did. I began going through some rough patches in my life." Jesus told Matthew I have always been there with you. In Deuteronomy 31:6, I will never leave you nor forsake you. I see everything you do and the things you've been going through. I also see the things you think I don't see. I know what you've been going through. Jesus said you had some idols that were more valuable than Me, and that was your job and money. They meant more to you than your family. Matthew didn't say a word because he knew Jesus was correct in everything He said.

Jesus then said to Matthew the bible states in Hebrew 13:5, "Keep your life free from love of money and be content with what you have for he has said." When He said that right there, Matthew felt loved by Jesus so much that tears began to roll down his face. Jesus told Matthew, "Don't worry, my son, everything will work out for you. I see you met Micheal. It was I who sent him down there to help you on earth. Micheal is one of my angels that sits next to me and my father. I will fix everything for you but, you will have to do your part, son." Matthew said, "I will, Lord." Then Jesus blew His breath in Matthew's face. Matthew looked up at the sky and saw that it was a bright morning with the sounds of birds chirping, and it was very quiet on the streets until Matthew heard someone call his name. Matthew!!! The voice shouted. Then the man shouted again, Matthew!!! He thought it was Jesus calling him again. Matthew looked up and saw Micheal's face. Matthew said, "Hey, Micheal, you're back from heaven too. Micheal said, "Well, I went home for the night, and I am back on the streets working for the Lord.

Let's go get you some clean clothes and something to eat." They went into a local clothing store. Matthew picked out a couple of outfits and a pair of sneakers. They walked up to the register to pay, and Micheal said to Matthew, "The money is in your pocket." Matthew reached into his pocket and couldn't believe somehow Micheal put the money in his pocket without him even knowing. He asked, how did you do that, Micheal. Micheal just smiled at Matthew. Matthew said I didn't even feel you put it in there. They then walked into a restaurant, and the waiter said may I take your order. Micheal said I don't want anything. Matthew asked, "Are you sure?" "Yes, you go ahead and order for yourself." The waiter was looking at Matthew as if he was talking to himself. Micheal said, "Enjoy yourself, don't worry about this old man." After Matthew finished eating, Micheal said I would like to take you to meet a very good friend of mine. His name is Gabriel; you

16

can stay with him.

They walked to this church that sat in the middle of nowhere. "You want me to stay here at some church?" Micheal said, "Yes, you can stay at the church until you get on your feet." So they walked up the steps together, and Matthew opened the big brown heavy doors. Micheal was right behind him, holding the door. When Matthew looked back, Micheal had vanished into thin air. Matthew looked all down the street, and Micheal was nowhere to be found. So Matthew proceeded to go inside the church. Matthew heard this noise in the church and saw this old man with pearly white hair walking down the aisle toward him. The man said, "Hello," Matthew said, "Hello, sir." "How are you doing?" "I am ok. My name is Matthew, and a friend of yours came here with me, but I don't know where he went. It's like he disappeared. His name is Michael. He said I could come here and receive some help from you." "Yes, of course, I was expecting you. I knew you were coming." Matthew said, "Oh, Micheal must've called you on the phone and told you all about me." "Nope," Gabriel said, "The Lord told me all about you." Then Gabriel smiled and said, "Follow me, Matthew, to the back of the church." They went to a little room that had a bed, nightstand, and a lamp. Next to the lamp was a bible that sat open.

Gabriel said, "It's not much but, I guess it will work for now. You can stay here as long as you like for free of charge." Matthew looked around astonishingly. Gabriel continued, "So, Matthew, tell me a little about yourself, and I will do the same." Matthew said, "Well, right now, I am homeless because I lost my job, and then my wife and daughter moved to another state. So I am here all alone. I have been wandering around the streets until I met your friend Micheal and he directed me here to you." Gabriel said, "You know Jesus truly loves you even though you may not feel He does at the times of your troubles. Matthew, don't give up on life because God never gave up on you." Matthew said, "You know you're right, Gabriel. Life has not been the best for me. My life was going so well for me, and I don't know what happened. It happened so fast.

At first, I had a lovely wife and daughter, and then she said she was leaving me because she said I worked too much." Gabriel asked, "Matthew, when was the last time you worshipped and prayed on your knees? How about studying your Bible? Basically, I am trying to tell you that God wants to spend time with you." "Well, it's been quite some time. I have been so caught up with work and being on many business trips. I just didn't have any spare time in my schedule." Gabriel said, "Now you have all the time in the world." "I kinda gave up on stuff because it's not working out for me, as you can see clearly the situation I am in.

My past came back to me, and I started drinking again. I haven't had a drink in over ten years. I was in my late teens when I became addicted to alcohol. My life is now turned upside down. I decided to turn back to drinking to help keep my mind off of all the problems I have been going through. If God truly loves me, why would He allow me to be homeless?" Gabriel said to Matthew, "God truly loves you, but you have your own free will. Matthew, have you ever tried praying with a sincere heart?" "Now come to think about it. I just pray a quick prayer. I thought by me praying that's good enough for God." Gabriel said to Matthew, "You have to pray to God with your whole heart and with intense prayers. You have to build a relationship with God. God will also restore what you have lost. I talk to God and spend countless times with him. That's the relationship God and I have together. That's what you are missing in your life. Well, Matthew, follow me and let me show you where you will be sleeping at." So they walked into this room. It only had a bed, *dresser*, a nightstand, and on the nightstand was a bible which sat open. Gabriel said, "Matthew, this is the room where I normally sleep but, don't worry, I have another room just down the hall. Do you need anything before I leave?" Gabriel was about to leave the room when Matthew said, "I really appreciate you for opening up your heart and room for me." "It's my pleasure, Matthew; you don't have to thank me. I am just doing the work of the Lord." Gabriel then added, "Read a scripture before you close your eyes." Matthew said, "I will think about it." Gabriel said, "You just might hear God's voice speak to you." Matthew laughed and said, "Gabriel, I have backslid against God. I don't think I am worthy enough." Gabriel said, "Yes, you are. Don't think less of yourself. I will return to you in the morning. Get yourself a *good* night's rest." Matthew said, "Ok, good night." So, Gabriel closed the door.

CHAPTER 4

Matthew's Visitation to heaven with Jesus

Matthew decided to go to sleep and was awakened by a deep stern voice. When the voice called his name, his heart began to pound so hard, and his hands were shaking uncontrollably. Matthew's body was so shaken up. Then the stern voice called him again, and then he sat up on his bed. Matthew said, "Whoever is there, show yourself to me."

Then Jesus appeared to Matthew like a bright light, and Matthew dropped to his knees worshipping the Lord. Jesus said. "Rise, my son, no need to be afraid." When Matthew got off his knees, he looked at Jesus and couldn't believe what he was seeing. Jesus said, "I love you so much." So, Matthew took his arms and wrapped them around Jesus. Instantly Matthew felt the love that was coming off of Jesus. Matthew began to cry, and Jesus wiped his tears from his eyes. Jesus said, "Son, come with me." Jesus and Matthew went into this lighted doorway to Heaven. Matthew was so amazed when he got to Heaven. Matthew said, "I love it here. It's so nice and bright and peaceful here. I wouldn't have to worry about any problems here." Jesus said, "No, son, you have a family that needs you." Matthew said to Jesus, "They walked out of my life, and I don't have anyone now. I have nothing now and nowhere to live or a job." Jesus looked at Matthew and said, "Matthew, you have to trust me. I will never leave you nor forsake you. (Hebrews 13:5) I love you, Matthew, I just want you to do my father's will, and everything you lost will be restored back to you. Everything will work out fine. You have to have faith in me that everything will work out for you."

Then these two angels appeared from out of nowhere. When Matthew looked around, he didn't see Jesus anymore. One of the angels put his arm underneath Matthew's left armpit, and the other angel took him under his other armpit. When they lifted Matthew up, he closed his eyes because he felt as though he was on a roller coaster ride. Matthew opened his eyes, and when he looked up, he was staring at the ceiling of his room. He was looking all around the room because he wanted to make sure he was in the room at the church. Matthew had pinched himself because he thought he was having a dream. It was 7:15 am, so Matthew got out of the bed and went to the sanctuary to pray. He kneeled down at one of the pews to pray. He began to pray and worship God and praise the Lord. The tears were rolling down his face as he was singing songs. Matthew picked up the Bible, opened it up, and started reading it. Gabriel walked into the sanctuary and started shining the pews. "Good morning," Matthew said. Gabriel replied, "How did you sleep. I hope it was comfortable enough for you?" "It sure was," Matthew said, "I had a dream last night, and you and Micheal were God's archangels." "Really?" Gabriel said and smiled as he was still shining the pews. Matthew said, "It felt so real, but, of course, it was just a dream. I feel so refreshed, as though I am a new person. I just want to be like you. You're such a calm person and always appear at peace. I am ready to do God's will and preach and teach the gospel. People in the world need to be healed and delivered and need to know who God is. I can't wait until my life changes. I am going to call my wife and daughter, and I will go from there." Matthew tried to call his wife from the church's phone, but she didn't answer. All he got was the answering machine. So he decided to go back into his room to lay down, and as he was lying down, he began thinking about his wife and daughter. He closed his eyes. Then, Jesus appeared to him in a vision. This time he wasn't startled when he saw Jesus. Jesus said, "Come with me, my son; I have something else for you to see." So Matthew got out the bed and followed Jesus.

CHAPTER 5

Jesus takes Matthew to Hell

Jesus took Matthew through this dark hot tunnel, and as they were traveling, Matthew began seeing fire and flames at the end of the tunnel. He started panicking until Jesus said, "Welcome to Hell." Matthew saw many people screaming and crying. They were saying, "I am sorry, Lord. Please give me another chance." Matthew even heard a man say, I preached and Prophesied in your name Jesus. Matthew asked Jesus, "Was he in Hell because he Preached and Prophesied in your name?" Jesus answered Matthew and said, "No, he preached and prophesied in my name but only for him to get the glory. He charged my people every time he spoke a word in their life. People came from all over the world to hear him preach, and he enjoyed that. He had members in his church that were homeless and without food to eat, and he refused to help them. He never offered them food or helped them with a place to live. He lived in a big mansion and drove very expensive cars. He didn't do the will of my father. If you see someone in need, you must help them. The book of (Matthew 22:39) says, "and the second is like unto it, thou shalt love thy neighbor as thyself." People ought not to love money more than

Me. Matthew then heard another person say to Jesus, "it's not my time to die. I want to be saved and go to heaven now." Jesus said he had time to repent of his sins. Many people came to him trying to get them saved, but he just said to them, I will do it on my own time when I am good and ready. Then he got into a car accident one morning on his way to work. A drunk driver hit him head-on, and he died instantly. The drunk driver went to jail and turned his life around. He got saved, and now he is preaching the Gospel in prison to the inmate. I cleaned him up, and now he is out of prison and preaching to inmates at different prisons. I look at the heart of man, not the outside of a person. Matthew looked to his left and saw people's skin melting off of their bodies like ice cream in the hot sun. The people couldn't run anywhere because the demons had their legs and arms chained up. Some were chained up, and some were trying to find a way to escape, but there was no way out of hell. Matthew asked Jesus, "Why do you bring me here?" Jesus said, "So that when you go back, you can tell your testimony about this place. My people need to know that hell is a real place. I want my people to know that I love them, and I don't want anyone to come to hell, even you, Matthew. I want you to preach the gospel in my name. I will give you the words to say. I want you to study the Bible, and you will find all your answers in there. Now, are you ready to return?" "I am ready; I am not trying to come back to this place ever again." Matthew and Jesus returned to the room at the church. When Matthew woke up out of the vision, he didn't see Jesus. Matthew jumped out of the bed, put his shoes on, and ran out of the room. He saw Gabriel in the sanctuary as usual. Matthew said, "Hello!" Gabriel asked Matthew, "Are you ok?" "Yes, I am fine." "You're in such a big hurry where you are off to?" "I am off to the streets to warn God's people of His return soon. He's coming back soon like a thief in the night." "You never know when He's coming." Matthew ran out of the church and went from door to door of people's homes, telling them about Jesus and His return soon. He even shared his own testimony about his life. There were a lot of people that didn't believe him and called him crazy, and told him to get away from their homes. There were some people who believed him. Matthew told people the warnings of hell and how it is a real place, and it's not a joke. While Matthew was taking a walk, he saw his friend, Jim. They began to talk, and Matthew told Jim his testimony about Heaven and then about how he had a visitation to hell. Jim actually believed Matthew. Jim said I saw your wife and daughter. They moved back into town. She asked me if I saw you and to tell you she's back, and she gave me her address to give to you. Matthew was so happy to hear that great news. Jim dropped Matthew off at the church. When Matthew got inside, he saw Gabriel, and he told him everything about heaven and that hell is a real place. He even told Gabriel about God's warning for God's people. Gabriel was so happy for Matthew because he was getting back on track.

CHAPTER 6

Matthew heals unclean spirits and diseases

Matthew woke up on Saturday morning, and he took the bus to his old neighborhood where he used to live with his wife and daughter. On his way, he saw this old homeless man in a wheelchair digging in a trash can. God spoke to Matthew and told him to give the man everything in his pocket. Matthew did, and he also started preaching to the man.

God then gave him instructions to heal the man. The man was very friendly, and Matthew began telling him about Jesus, then God spoke suddenly to Matthew again and told him to lay his hands on the man's legs. Matthew said to the man, "God wants to heal you. He wants you out of that wheelchair and set free." The man said, "I have been in this wheelchair for over 25 years. I fought in the Vietnam war, and I was shot in my legs and in my lower back, and it paralyzed me from the waist down. I used to do the same thing you're doing now when I was away fighting for our country. I would preach and preach to a lot of people. One of our generals even received Jesus. We would be up late at night rejoicing in the Lord. Then unexpectedly, one day, out of nowhere, these men came out and shot me. When that happened,

I became very depressed. I was married and have three children. When I came home, the whole house was empty. My wife and kids were gone. When I peeked inside, there wasn't anything inside. It was all cleaned out. To top it off, it was a sold sign outside on the lawn. When I was away, I would send her my whole paycheck. So she can take care of the kids and bills. I never once mistreat her in any way. I love her and my children." Matthew said, "God will heal your broken heart. Let me pray for you, sir." So Matthew laid his hands on the man in the wheelchair.

God spoke in Matthew's ear and told him what words to say. Then immediately, the man felt a warm feeling going down his lower body. He began to praise the Lord and cry. Then Matthew said, sir, please stand up, and he did. He stood up and moved both of his legs like never before. The man just couldn't believe that he was totally healed, and he kept praising the Lord. He also, Thanked Matthew so much for obeying the Lord's commandments. Matthew said to the man, "I must go now. Remember to study and pray. God loves you always." Matthew walked down the street to his old house. It had a for sale sign on the lawn.

He looked inside the house and saw a vision of him and his wife and daughter. Then as Matthew was out of the vision, he couldn't believe his eyes of what he was seeing. So he went to the door and turned the knob on the front door. When the door opened, he saw all these bright specks falling like rain in the house. They were all over Matthew, and then angels appeared everywhere. Then this big bright light came from the upstairs. Jesus appeared from the upstairs and said, "Your life has been restored." Then all the specks of lights, even Jesus, disappeared. Matthew left the house and walked down the street, not really understanding what Jesus meant. Matthew knew right there it was time for a change in his life.

CHAPTER 7

Matthew makes a surprise visit

Matthew walked down the street and went to Jim's house, and knocked on the door. "Good morning, Jim, Can you take me to see my family?" Immediately Jim said yes. So they got into Jim's car and left. They came to this blue house in the country part of Georgia.

The house sat on seven acres of land with a pretty all-white horse in the fence. Matthew noticed a child on the all-white horse and a woman with a pink hat holding her up. Matthew said to Jim, that's Racheal and Katie. Jim said it sure is, Matthew. So he said, "Jim, please stop the car!!!" Matthew jumped out of the car and ran, shouting Racheal and Katie's names. All you can do is hear Katie say, daddy!!!! Racheal hugged Matthew so tight she didn't want to let him go. Jim yelled from the car and said, "I'll see you later, man, enjoy yourself with your family. I will come back later on to get you." Matthew said, "Ok, thanks so much, man."

Matthew turned around and picked Katie off the ground and swung her around. Racheal said, "Honey, this was my grandma's house, and she passed away last year and left it to me. Matthew said, "Well, let me be honest to you. I lost my job and everything else. I lost the car and the house we worked so hard saving our money to get. The worst part is I am homeless, but now I am sleeping at a church that belongs to a good friend of mine. He stays there too and keeps the place clean. He has been helping me through my journey. There's another good man that's been helping me through this journey too, and his name is Micheal. You have to meet them. You will love them both." Rachael said, "Don't worry, the things you lost God can replace them back. Those things are just materialistic things that can be replaced.

They all went inside to have a bite to eat. Racheal made Matthew's favorite, a grilled chicken sandwich with the works and a fresh glass of lemonade juice. They sat on the porch and laughed for hours about old time's memories. Racheal invited Matthew back to stay the next day. Matthew said, "I need to talk to God first, honey. I learned not to make any moves without God first." Just as Matthew was going to call Jim, he was coming down the road. Jim drove Matthew back to the church and dropped Matthew off.

Matthew ran into the church and looked into Gabriel's room. Gabriel was in there kneeled down praying, but when Matthew walked all the way into Gabriel's room, he saw Jesus, and the room was so lighted up. Jesus was there, giving the angels and Gabriel instructions. Matthew was so shocked at what he saw. Then Jesus spoke and acknowledged Matthew. Jesus said, "Matthew, you have been a great servant for Me. So I will soon reward you. I have called you to be my prophet and my mouthpiece." Matthew just couldn't believe what Jesus said. Jesus added, "I know your heart." Matthew then left the room and went to bed with a smile on his face.

The next day was a Sunday morning. Matthew called Racheal and told her to meet him at their home church. Matthew spotted Katie coming into the church with Racheal hopping on one foot. Then he saw his wife dressed up in an all-white dress. The pastor of the church began preaching, and after he was done preaching, he asked if there were anyone that wanted to be saved or dedicate their life back to the Lord. The tears began to flow from Matthew's eyes, and Rachael began to cry when she saw the tears from her husband's eyes. When he looked up, the pastor anointed his head and prayed for Matthew. Immediately, Matthew fell out in the spirit. Matthew saw Gabriel on Jesus' left and Micheal on his right side.

They all hugged Matthew and said to him, "You did well. We will miss you on earth, but we will always be with you." Then Jesus put His hands on Matthew's head, and when he opened his eyes, there were church members around him. Matthew stood up with a great smile on his face as he looked at everyone with great amazement. Matthew started telling everyone his testimony about meeting Jesus and God's Archangels. He also told the people that God called him to be His Prophet. The look on the people's faces was so shocking. Matthew stood up and started praying for different people in the church that had canes and was in wheelchairs. Matthew prophesied to the pastor and his wife of the church. He told them that God saw that they were trying to have a baby, and God said she shall conceive within six months. Nobody knew this but her and her husband. Matthew Prophesied to this older man in his sixties that had cancer. He told him God had healed him from that.

The pastor of the church couldn't believe what he was hearing. The Holy Spirit was flowing in the church, so strong people were worshipping and crying out to God. Matthew then said to the pastor, you've been going through some financial difficulties, but God said cast thy burdens upon the Lord and he shall sustain thee. He shall never suffer the righteous to be moved Psalms 55:22).

The pastor knew that God was speaking through Matthew because he didn't share any of his information with anyone, not even his wife. Matthew later left the church service with his wife and daughter. He told Racheal he was going to stop by and see Gabriel. When he got there, it was a black man there wiping down the pews and singing holy holy holy.

So Matthew walked up to the man and said, "Hello. How are you doing? I am looking for Gabriel. Have you seen him?" The man said, "I am Joe. I haven't seen anyone by that name come by here. I have been working here cleaning this church for over 40 years." Now Matthew was looking like he was lost. Matthew asked Joe if he can go into the room where Gabriel sleeps. Joe said, "Go right ahead." So Matthew opened the door, and it was an empty storage closet. Then he went into the room where he was sleeping, and that room was completely empty. Joe walked up behind Matthew and said I told you, young man, nobody was in there. Joe started laughing. Matthew thanked Joe and left out the church. Matthew was wondering what in the world was going on. Matthew was hoping to see Micheal, but he didn't. Matthew walked past this building when he heard God's voice say to him go inside. So he went into the tall building with tinted windows. The lady said, "May I help you, sir?" Matthew said, "Hi!" "I know you," the lady said with a big smile on her face, "We worked together before at the other company before they laid everybody off.

Let me guess you're here to fill in the other open position." Matthew looked at her with a shocking look on his face. "Yes, I guess," Matthew said, "I didn't bring my resumes." She said, "Don't worry about that." She walked into this office and introduced Matthew to her boss. The lady told him all about Matthew, and the man said, "Well, you're hired. I will see you tomorrow." Matthew said, "Of course," then he walked back to the front desk and thanked the lady. She said to Matthew, God speaks to me too. Matthew said to her I will see you tomorrow morning.

When Matthew walked out of the building, he saw Micheal and Gabriel. Matthew said, "Hey, guys. Please tell the truth about what's going on." They both just laughed together. Gabriel said, "Ok, Micheal and I were sent down here by the Lord. We helped you by sending people your way and helping your life get better. Now that you have everything you need, including your wife and daughter. We are going back home to our dwelling place to be with the Lord and completing our assignments for God. We have so many more people that are in need of our help." Then Matthew noticed as they were walking that people were walking through them. Micheal turned around with a smile and said, "We are heavenly angels. People can't see us; only you can." Then the sky lit up, and the people that were walking were blinded by the bright light that shone from the sky. Gabriel and Micheal had disappeared into the sky. Matthew's phone rang, and it was Rachael on the other end.

Matthew said to his wife, "Honey, I am coming home for good. Can you come and get me from the coffee shop downtown Atlanta. I will be waiting there." She said to Matthew, I am on my way. Matthew, his wife, and daughter prayed everyday together, and on Saturdays, they devoted their time preaching and teaching on the streets.

About The Author

Author Enile Hargett is a dedicated writer and a woman that loves the Lord. Enile is very passionate about the Lord. She is a mother with seven children and one grandson. She obeyed God and was obedient to her assignment, and this book is the manifestation of her faith in God. The Lord told the author that this will be a sermon in the book. God birthed out of her, "Put God first."

This is her life's testimony.

To contact the Author Enile Hargett

Email: enile.hargett@yahoo.com

www.ingramcontent.com/pod-product-compliance
Lightning Source LLC
Chambersburg PA
CBHW071950100426
42736CB00042B/2680